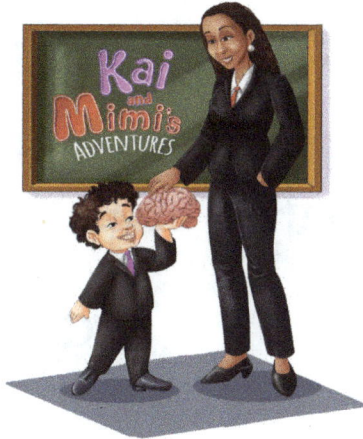

©2024 Kimberly L. Suber and Kai A. Suber

All rights reserved.

Illustrator: Kreative Artz

Published by: Kai and Mimi's Adventures

info@kaiandmimi.org

Kai's Brainventure with Mimi Quick Reference Guide

ISBN: 979-8-9903372-2-0

Ebook ISBN: 979-8-9903372-3-7

> "We must recognize that trauma holds immense power and takes precedence over everything else."
>
> **Kimberly L. Suber**

As parents, educators, caregivers, and mentors, it is vital to approach each child as a unique individual and equip them with the necessary skills for success. "Kai's Brainventure with Mimi" serves as a valuable resource for learning how to engage with children from a young age to foster their emotional security and regulation. This guide serves as a tool to comprehend the reasons behind varying student responses and offers insights into providing interventions when they are emotionally unregulated.

SKILLS OVERVIEW: ACES or Adverse Childhood Experiences and Trauma, The Effects of Trauma, Brain Research and Facts, Interventions, and Neurological Attachments with Caregivers.

What are adverse childhood experiences?

Adverse childhood experiences (ACEs) such as abuse, neglect, and family dysfunction occurring from birth to age 18 can impede brain development and restrict social, emotional, and cognitive abilities. These experiences often underlie various significant academic, social, and behavioral challenges that may hinder a child from fully capitalizing on educational opportunities.

Reduces the ability to respond, learn, or figure things out, which can result in problems in school.

Increases difficulty in making friends and maintaining relationships.

Increases stress hormones which affect the body's ability to fight infection.

Lowers tolerance for stress, which can result in behaviors such as fighting, checking out or defiance.

May cause lasting health problems.

Increases problems with learning and memory which can be permanent.

Experiences can commence as early as infancy, underscoring the significance of offering children constructive experiences that will shape their cognitive development.

Identifying Trauma

What is Trauma? It is the emotional response to a terrible event that is either witnessed or experienced by the individual. The event overwhelms the person's ability to cope and cause feelings of fear, helplessness or horror, which may be expressed by disorganized or agitated behavior.

The Original 10 ACES (Adverse Childhood Experiences)

ABUSE: ....

Physical   Emotional   Sexual

NEGLECT: ....

Physical   Emotional

HOUSEHOLD CHALLENGES: ....

Divorce   Incarceration   Substance Use

Domestic Violence   Mental Illness

Beyond the 10 ACEs

Discrimination

Poverty

Racism

Other Violence

Intergenerational and Cultural Trauma

Separation

Adjustment or Other Major Life Changes

Bereavement or Survivorship

Adult Responsibilities As A Child

Trauma and Social Location

An individual's trauma encompasses more than their personal experiences. Children enter a world shaped by pre-existing structures and circumstances. These frameworks frequently adopt punitive measures, such as zero-tolerance policies within educational settings, intertwined with inherent racial prejudices. As a result, these structures constrain opportunities and perpetuate economic and social disparities.

Adverse Childhood Experiences

01
02
03
04
05

Scientific Gaps

Death

Conception

Trauma and Social Location

Historical Trauma and Embodiment

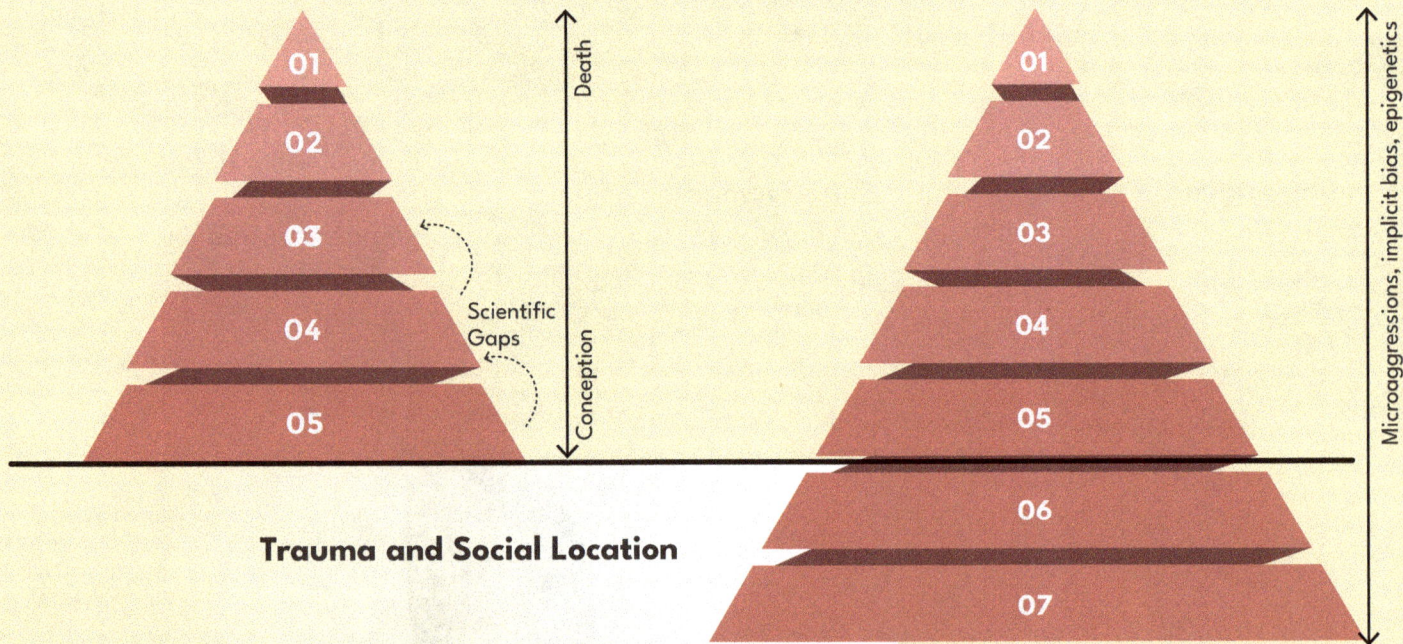

01
02
03
04
05
06
07

Microaggressions, implicit bias, epigenetics

01 Early Death

02 Disease, Disability and Social Problems

03 Adoption of Health- Risk Behaviors

04 Social, Emotional and Cognitive Impairment

05 Adverse Childhood Experiences

01 Early Death

02 Burden of disease, distress, criminalization, and stigmatization

03 Coping

04 Disrupted Neurological Development

05 Complex Trauma/ACE

06 Social Conditions/ Local Context

07 Generational Embodiment/ Historical Trauma

6

Two Types of Trauma

1 **Simple Trauma:**
Usually associated with a singular event.

- Clear commencement and conclusion.
- After the event, individuals can usually find safety, stability, access help, and initiate recovery.
- Example: A standalone car accident.

2 **Complex Trauma:**
Involves persistent or frequently recurring incidents.

- Involves multiple traumatic episodes.
- Lack of a distinct endpoint.
- Safety, stability, and recovery can appear unattainable.

Impact of Childhood Trauma

Behavior
- Poor self-regulation
- Social withdrawal
- Aggression
- Poor impulse control
- Risk-taking/illegal activity
- Sexual acting out
- Adolescent pregnancy
- Drug and alcohol misuse

Cognition
- Impaired readiness
- Difficulty problem-solving
- Language Delays
- Problems with concentration
- Poor academic achievement

Physical Health
- Sleep disorders
- Eating disorders
- Poor immune system functioning
- Cardiovascular disease
- Shorter life span

Brain Development
- Smaller brain size
- Less efficient processing
- Impaired stress response
- Changes in gene expression

Mental Health
- Depression
- Anxiety
- Negative self-image/ low self-esteem
- PTSD Disorder
- Suicidal

Emotions
- Difficulty controlling emotions
- Trouble recognizing emotions
- Limited coping skills
- Increased sensitivity to stress
- Shame and guilt
- Excessive worry and hopelessness
- Feelings of helplessness/lack of self- efficacy

Relationships
- Attachment problems/disorders
- Poor understanding of social interactions
- Difficulty forming relationships with peers
- Problems in romantic relationships
- Intergenerational cycles of abuse

The Effects of Complex Trauma

Attachment and Relationships:

- Challenges in forming secure and healthy attachments
- Struggles with regulating and articulating emotions effectively
- Display of violent or inappropriate responses to various situations

Emotional Responses:

- Challenges in recognizing, articulating, and regulating emotions
- Displaying defensive behaviors
- Experiencing emotional numbing

Behavior:

- Prone to being easily triggered or provoked
- Difficulty in self-regulation
- Impaired impulse control
- Exhibits unpredictability, oppositional behavior, and volatility
- Tends to engage in high-risk activities

Self-Concept & Future Orientation:

- Self-attribution of blame for experienced abuse
- Prevalence of shame and guilt
- Low self-esteem
- Negative self-image
- Absence of a sense of competence
- Pessimistic outlooks

Physical Health:

- Compromised immune system
- Inconsistent responses to stress
- Enduring physical ailments
- Dysregulation of bodily functions
- Persistent experience of chronic pain

Dissociation:

- Engaging in mental detachment from the situation
- Sensations of disconnection from one's body

Cognition (Thinking & Learning):

- Struggles with problem-solving and reasoning
- Lacks the ability to plan ahead and execute plans effectively
- Encounters challenges in acquiring new skills
- Demonstrates attention deficits

Long-Term Health Implications:

- Manifestation of chronic illnesses, including heart disease and cancer
- Premature mortality

Behaviors and Indicators of Trauma

Lying	Avoidance and self-protection
Back-talking	Control Seeking
Running Away	Avoidance and/ or flight response
Defiance	Control-seeking
Hyperactivity	Anxiety and/or hypervigilance
Property Destruction	Fight response
Physical Aggression	Fight Response
Stealing	Thrill-seeking/impulse control
Self-harming behaviors (ex: cutting)	Unhealthy coping skills
Not listening or remember directions	Undeveloped executive functioning skills
Temper tantrums at any age	Control-seeking/undeveloped executive functioning skills

How to respond to students affected by trauma?

▶ Practice non-judgmental listening

▶ Engage in active listening

▶ Foster a safe and supportive environment

▶ Offer de-escalation strategies

▶ Respect their pace in processing emotions; recovery takes time

▶ Avoid administering an ACE survey during this time

▶ Maintain consistency in interactions

▶ Encourage educators to incorporate brain breaks or provide support as needed

▶ Cultivate resilience

▶ Lead by example consistently

Let's go on a Brainventure

What is the brain?

The brain, serving as the powerful conductor of our bodies, resembles a high-performance supercomputer that coordinates all our actions, thoughts, and emotions. Comprised of miniature brain cells known as neurons, it transmits rapid messages to maintain our coordination. From defining our identity to igniting our ideas and emotions, the brain emerges as our individual champion, crafting our distinct personalities.

Prefrontal Cortex

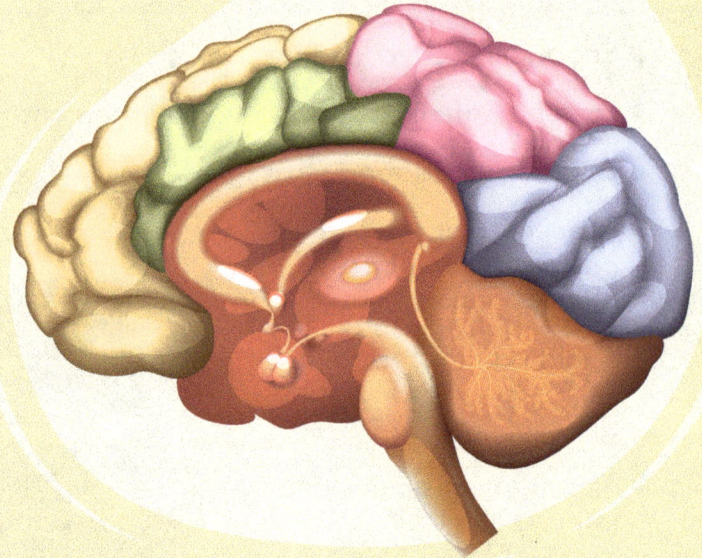

Amygdala

Hippocampus

Delving into the Mysteries of the Mind

Various brain sections are like a bustling team, each with its own unique role - from pondering and wiggling to feeling the feels and managing life-sustaining tasks like breathing and heartbeats. Today's spotlight is on three brain VIPs: the Prefrontal Cortex, the Amygdala, and the Hippocampus.

The prefrontal cortex (PFC) is situated at the front of the brain and plays a crucial role in cognition, decision-making, and emotional processing. This region aids in memory retention, concentration, and impulse control. As we acquire new knowledge, the PFC adjusts its neural connections, enabling us to adapt and react more effectively to various circumstances. **"The Wise Owl"**

Just as the wise owl symbolizes wisdom, the prefrontal cortex acts as the intelligent decision-maker in our brain. This part of the brain aids in critical thinking, strategizing, and making sound decisions. Similar to the sharp intellect of an owl, it manages higher-order cognitive functions effectively.

The **amygdala**, located in the temporal lobe, is a brain structure shaped like an almond. It plays a crucial role in managing emotions, particularly fear, and is essential for memory and motivation as a component of the limbic system.

Significance: Think of the amygdala as your own personal guard dog, always on high alert to sniff out any potential danger. Just like a loyal pup protecting its turf, the amygdala is the emotional powerhouse in your brain, especially when it comes to fear and intense feelings. By swiftly reacting to risky situations or emotional rollercoasters, it's like having a built-in safety net for your emotions.

BEWARE OF THE DOG

The **hippocampus**, chilling in the brain's tempo lobes, rocks a seahorse vibe. This area is the memory maestro, pulling strings to turn short-term memories into long-lasting hits! **"The Memory Elephant"**

The hippocampus is often compared to a memory elephant due to its vital role in learning and memory. Similar to elephants' remarkable memory abilities in recalling locations and experiences over extended periods, the hippocampus plays a key role in establishing and strengthening long-term memories. Serving as the brain's memory hub, it transforms short-term memories into long-lasting ones and aids in spatial navigation, mirroring elephants' capacity to remember extensive territories and traverse through them.

Left versus Right
Verbal Expression versus Emotions

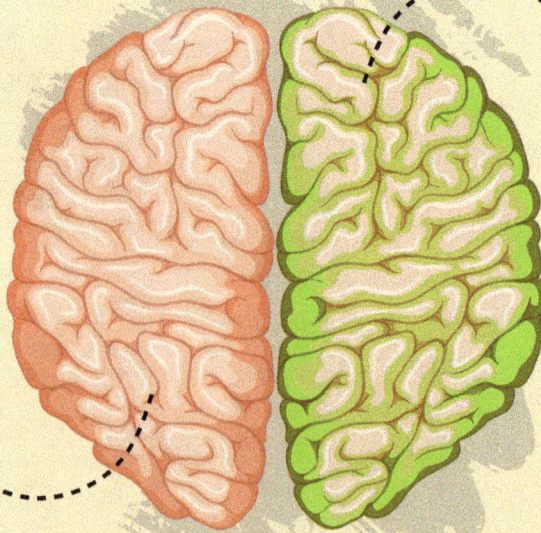

Left Hemisphere

- Sensory Stimulus from right side of body
- Motor control of right side of body
- Speech, language and comprehension
- Analysis and calculations,
- Time and sequencing
- Recognition of words, letters and numbers

Right Hemisphere

- Sensory stimulus from left side of body
- Motor control of left side of body
- Creativity
- Spatial ability
- Context/perception
- Recognition of faces places and objects

How does trauma impact the brain?

Thinking Brain

▶ The "Green Brain" transitions into the "Thinking Brain."

▶ It is responsible for strategizing and resolving issues.

▶ Cultivates mindfulness among individuals.

▶ Engages in the processing of information derived from words, concepts, and thoughts.

▶ Focuses on scrutinizing specific details.

Feeling and Reacting Brain

▶ Yellow Brain represents the Feeling & Reacting Brain

▶ It involves being in a heightened emotional state

▶ Reacting based on emotions rather than logic/reasoning

▶ There may be a loss of control over responses

▶ Strong emotional experiences, but not feeling psychologically unsafe

Survival Brain

▶ The Red Brain shifts to the Survival Brain

▶ It becomes active upon encountering a triggering stimulus

▶ Primarily addresses imminent dangers

▶ Operates swiftly

▶ Prioritizes sensory input

▶ Lacks focus on specifics

▶ Disregards verbal cues

▶ Triggers Fight, Flight, or Freeze reactions

Your Upstairs Brain

- Create a fist with your hand, and voilà!
- You've just crafted your very own brain.
- In this brainy abode, there's an upstairs and a downstairs - like a fancy duplex for your thoughts.
- The Upstairs Brain is your wise owl, guiding you to make stellar choices even when the storm clouds of emotions roll in.

The Ok Brain

- Form an "OK" hand sign to symbolize the brain's caution zone.
- Feeling blue is A-OK!
- It's just a brain blip.
- Give those fingers a squeeze and watch the Upstairs Brain high-five your thumb.
- Keeping it cool downstairs when the Upstairs Brain is in a tizzy can be a real game-changer.

Your Downstairs Brain

- Ready, set, give those fingers a tiny lift!
- Check out where your thumb lands.
- That's where your Downstairs Brain lives.
- It's the cozy home of your Big Feelings.
- Big feelings like love, care, and a sprinkle of grumpiness spring from this magical spot!

Brain and Stress Facts

1 **The brain is dynamic, constantly adapting to its surroundings, much like the versatile nature of a chameleon.**

2 Early stressful or traumatic events can directly influence a child's brain development.

3 The brain undergoes significant changes in the initial five years, with a particular focus on the period from birth to age three. This critical phase exposes the brain and its neural pathways to external influences.

4 Persistent stress can have adverse effects on learning, development, and behavior.

5 **When we perceive a threat, our body triggers the stress response systems and releases stress hormones such as adrenaline and cortisol.**

6 The purpose of stress reactions and chemicals is to safeguard us; however, an excess can lead to the opposite outcome.

7 Prolonged activation of stress response systems during early childhood can disturb the brain's structure and its communication with the body, potentially resulting in significant health problems later on.

8 **The brain reaches full development between the ages of 22 to 24, varying by gender.**

Neurological Attachment

- During infancy, the brain is only a quarter of its adult size.
- The development of the brain is significantly influenced by the child's initial attachment relationship, which is socially constructed.
- A nurturing adult's interactions, conveyed through eye contact and facial expressions, play a crucial role in programming an infant's brain.
- Early intervention in a child's life impacts their development, genetic expression, and the neural plasticity of the brain.
- The critical period for neuroplasticity spans from birth to five years of age.
- In infancy, the brain establishes approximately 1,000 connections per second, a rate unparalleled in any other developmental stage.

Emotional Glue

Babies require emotional bonding for future attachments to develop. The foundation of these attachments lies in the reciprocal interactions between the baby and their caregiver. Reciprocity involves responding to the infant's gaze and participating in meaningful conversations.

Developing Attachments

▶ The foundation of secure attachment is established when children perceive the caregiver as accessible and capable, themselves as deserving of care, and the world as a safe place.

▶ Security fosters self-regulation. Feeling secure enables children to confidently explore their surroundings, with the assurance of a safe haven to return to. Even in times of confusion, timely intervention can help children regulate their emotions effectively.

The Impact of Trauma on Children's Educational Preparedness

Language and Communication

▶ Language development delays and challenges

▶ Difficulties with expressive (e.g., expressing thoughts and feelings) and receptive language (e.g. understanding nonverbal cues)

▶ Difficulties with nonverbal communication (e.g., eye contact)

▶ Use of hurtful language (e.g., to keep others at a distance)

Language Facts

1 **Caregivers who cannot interact with children to encourage collaboration may hinder the development of an enriched vocabulary.**

2 Persistent states of heightened arousal can make it challenging for individuals to learn how to express themselves.

3 Transferring information between hemispheres facilitates the blending of words and emotions.

4 The integration between the left and right hemispheres is additionally hindered by trauma triggers that stimulate memories in the right hemisphere while diminishing the executive functions of the left side.

5 **Children who struggle with interactive and cooperative communication, like those with early trauma backgrounds, often face isolation or rejection by their peers.**

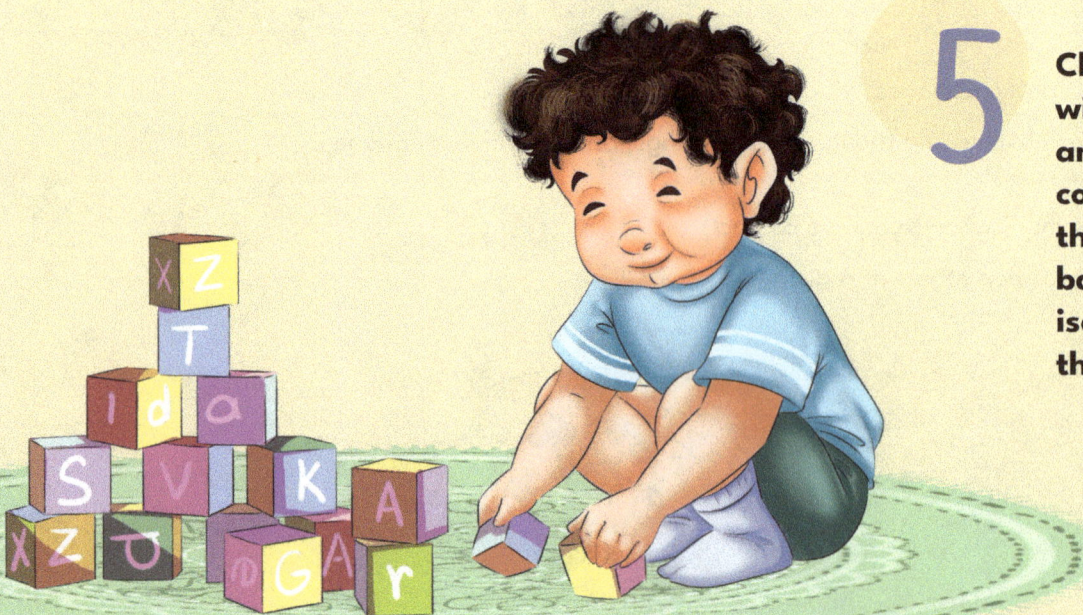

6 People experiencing stress may find it challenging to interpret body language and facial expressions.

7 Their silence is frequently perceived as sullen or defiant, yet it is actually a physiological response to stress.

8 **Stress-induced hormones like cortisol can hinder productivity, causing students to feel "lost for words."**

The Effects of Trauma

Attention

▶ Interactions with caregivers shape the brain's anticipation of specific experiences.

▶ In cases of chronic stress or trauma, individuals are conditioned to prioritize survival by focusing their attention on it.

Memory

▶ Implicit and explicit memory hold significant importance.

▶ Implicit memories develop during infancy; neglected children may face challenges in social and academic aspects.

▶ Explicit memories start to form around the age of two.

Executive Function

▶ The pre-frontal cortex acts as the brain's executive director. It matures over time to regulate the lower regions of the brain.

Inhibitory Control, Working Memory, and Cognitive Flexibility

▶ Inhibitory Control: Emphasize delayed gratification and managing impulses.

▶ Working Memory: Temporarily holds memories before transferring them to long-term storage.

▶ Cognitive Flexibility: Encourage thinking creatively and beyond conventional boundaries. It can be difficult to shift someone's mindset when they are consistently in survival mode.

Window of Tolerance Trauma/Anxiety Related Responses

Widening the Comfort Zone for Increased Flexibility

Hyper-Aroused
Fight/Flight Response

- Anxiety
- Overwhelmed
- Chaotic Responses
- Outbursts (Emotional or Aggressive)

- Anger/Aggression/Rage, Rigidness
- Obsessive Compulsive Behavior or Thoughts
- Over-Eating/Restricting

- Addictions
- Impulsivity

Causes To Go Out Of The Window Of Tolerance

Fear of......

- Unconscious Thought & Bodily Feeling Control, Unsafe I do not exist, Abandonment, Rejection

Trauma-Related Core Beliefs about self are triggered:

- Emotional & Physiological Dysregulation Occurs

Widening the window for psychological flexibility

Comfort Zone Emotionally Regulated

Calm, Cool, Collected, Connected

Ability To Self-Soothe Ability To Regulate Emotional State

Staying within the window allows for better relationship interactions

To Stay In the Window Of Tolerance

- Mindfulness: Being Present in Here-n-Now
- Grounding Exercises
- Techniques for Self-Soothing, Calming the Body & Emotional Regulation
- Deep Slow Breathing
- Recognize Limiting Beliefs, Counter with Positive Statements About Self, New Choices

Hypo-Aroused
Freeze Response

- Feign Death Response
- Dissociation
- Not Present

- Unavailable/Shut Down
- Memory Loss
- Disconnected

- Auto Pilot
- No Display of Emotions/Flat
- Separation From Self, Feelings and Emotions

Created by: Dan Siegel

Strategies for Children at Home and School

Calming Tools, Kits, and Spaces: Foster emotional regulation within the classroom by offering calming resources such as stress balls, small slinkies, thinking putty, an expanding ball, and glitter jars. Encourage students to utilize these tools within the classroom setting, promoting the normalization of emotional regulation without the need for students to leave the room.

Lighting Adjustment: Enhance the classroom environment by replacing harsh fluorescent lighting with full-spectrum light bulbs and utilizing curtains to soften the illumination from fluorescent fixtures, reducing visual noise.

Visual Aids and Signage: Improve communication within the classroom by prominently displaying clear, concise, and positive signage that is easily comprehensible for students. Opt for visually uncluttered designs that combine images and text effectively.

Noise Management: Create a conducive learning atmosphere by minimizing unnecessary noise disruptions within the classroom.

Temperature Control: Maintain a comfortable ambient temperature of approximately 72°F to support optimal student performance. If adjusting the temperature proves challenging, permit students to wear additional layers for personal comfort.

Environmental Concerns for Supportive Classrooms

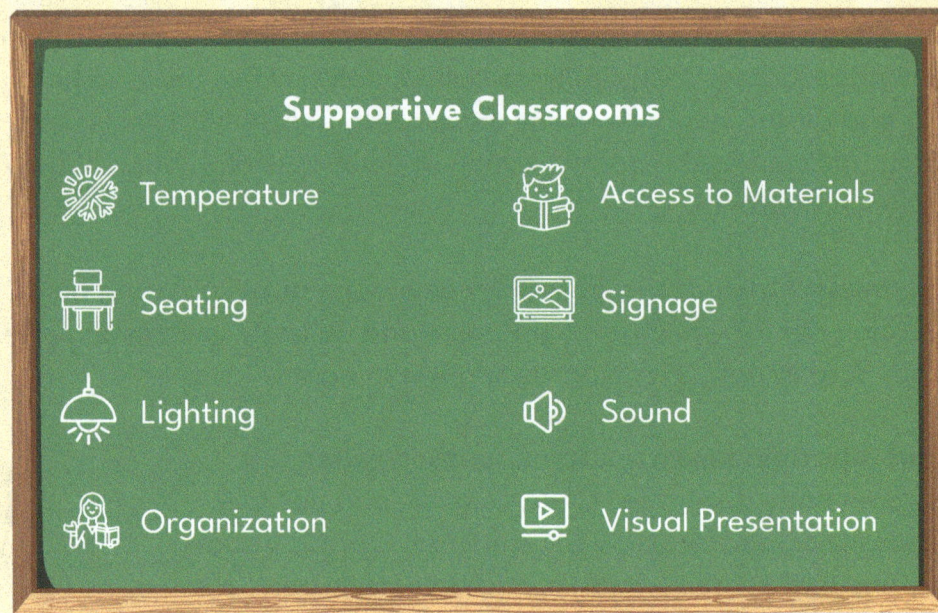

Supportive Classrooms

- Temperature
- Seating
- Lighting
- Organization
- Access to Materials
- Signage
- Sound
- Visual Presentation

References

Craig, S. E. (2016). Trauma-Sensitive Schools: Learning Communities Transforming Children's Lives, K-5. New York, NY: Teachers College Press.

Felitti, V. J., Anda, R. F., Nordenberg, D., Williamson, D. F., Spitz, A. M., Edwards, V., Koss, M. P., & Marks, J. S. (1998). Relationship of childhood abuse and household dysfunction to many of the leading causes of death in adults: The Adverse Childhood Experiences (ACE) Study. American Journal of Preventive Medicine, 14(4), 245–258.

Siegel, D. J. (1999). The developing mind: Toward a neurobiology of interpersonal experience. Guilford Press.

Siegel, D. J., & Payne Bryson, T. (2011). The whole-brain child: 12 revolutionary strategies to nurture your child's developing mind.

Glossary of Terminology

▶ **Downstairs Brain:** The foundational part of the brain responsible for managing emotions and vital functions such as breathing. It triggers responses like fight, flight, freeze, or fold.

▶ **Explicit Memory:** The ability to recall facts and skills, such as remembering a phone number or mathematical procedures.

▶ **Implicit Memory:** Memories derived from experiences that influence or shape our emotional responses.

▶ **Left Brain:** The analytical hemisphere of the brain involved in language development, reasoning, and the retention of factual information.

▶ **Neuroplasticity:** The brain's remarkable capacity to adapt, change, and form new neural connections.

▶ **Regulated:** The process of managing and responding to emotions effectively.

▶ **Right Brain:** The creative and intuitive hemisphere of the brain that fosters social interaction, imagination, motor skills, and exploration.

▶ **Social Organ:** The brain's need for social interactions, such as smiles and hugs, as it is inherently wired for social engagement.

▶ **Stimulating Activity:** Engaging and interactive experiences that aim to captivate and stimulate a child's senses, curiosity, and cognitive abilities.

▶ **Upstairs Brain:** The prefrontal cortex responsible for executive functions, preparing the brain for learning and higher-order thinking.

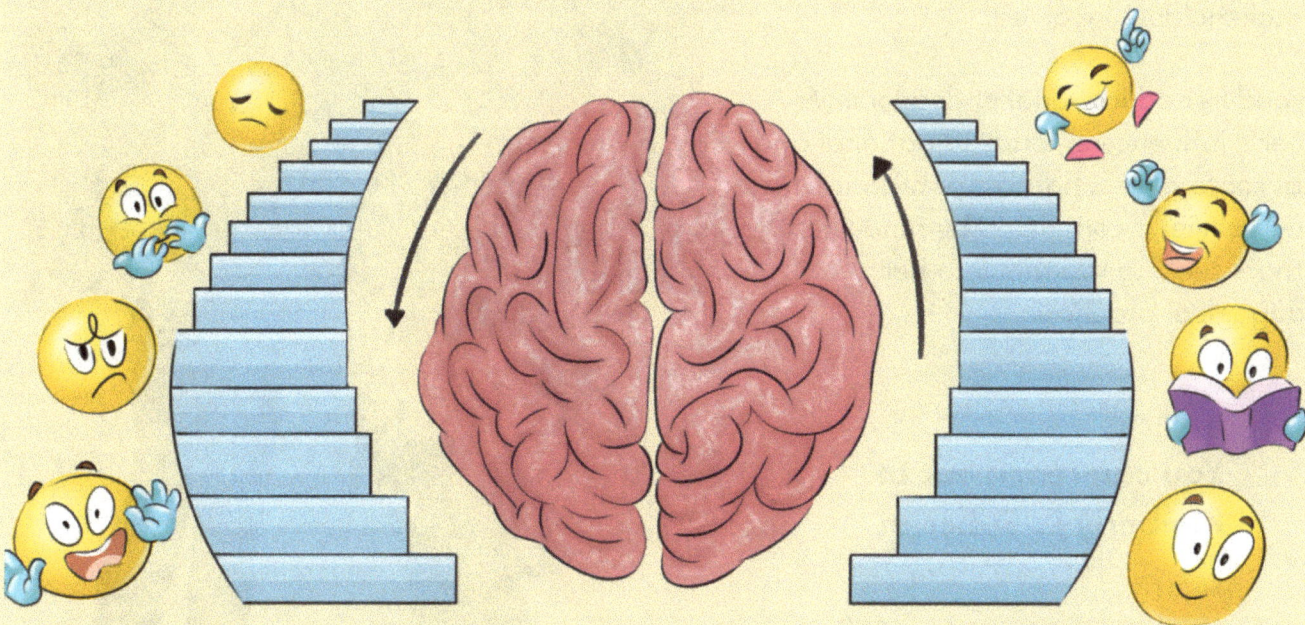

About the Authors

Kai Ashton Suber, widely recognized as Boss Baby, derives great joy from acquiring cognitive strategies under the guidance of his exceptional Mimi. Known for his infectious smile and exuberant expressions of delight upon each new discovery, Kai's enthusiasm resonates across the cosmos.

With an extensive background spanning over two decades in the field of education, Ms. Kimberly L. Suber has seamlessly transitioned through various roles, from teacher, to assistant principal, district administrator, and consultant. Ms. Suber stands as the visionary behind frameworks and methodologies dedicated to fostering academic motivation in children while addressing their Social and Emotional Learning requirements.

An ardent advocate of employing a positive behavior model supported by clear and consistent expectations to cultivate a secure educational environment, Ms. Suber envisions a setting where every child progresses towards their social and academic objectives. She ardently contributes to initiatives aimed at instigating positive transformations within educational institutions, benefiting all stakeholders involved.

Beyond her educational endeavors, Ms. Suber's influence extends to national and local conferences, notable publications, and interviews conducted by renowned authors seeking insights into her pedagogical practices.

You can reach out to Kimberly L. Suber at 864-590-4995 or info@kaiandmimi.org for speaking engagements and professional growth opportunities.

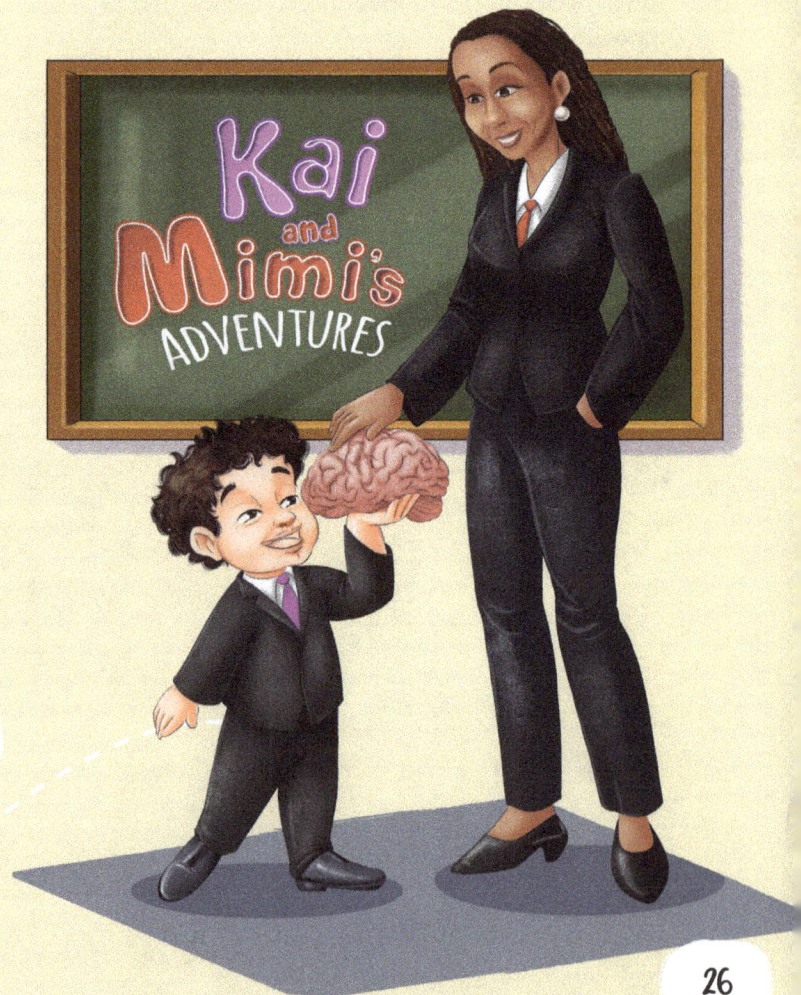

Notes

....

....

....

....

....

....

....

....

....

....

....

....

....

....

....

Notes

Notes

Notes

....

....

....

....

....

....

....

....

....

....

....

....

....

....

....

....

Notes

....

....

....

....

....

....

....

....

....

....

....

....

....

....

....

Notes

....

....

....

....

....

....

....

....

....

....

....

....

....

....